**W9-AUU-348**

# SQUIRRELS

## Tom Jackson

**Grolier**
an imprint of
**SCHOLASTIC**
www.scholastic.com/librarypublishing

Published 2008 by Grolier
An imprint of Scholastic Library Publishing
Old Sherman Turnpike, Danbury,
Connecticut 06816

**For The Brown Reference Group plc**
Project Editor: Jolyon Goddard
Copy-editors: Lesley Ellis, Lisa Hughes,
    Wendy Horobin
Picture Researcher: Clare Newman
Designers: Jeni Child, Lynne Ross,
    Sarah Williams
Managing Editor: Bridget Giles

Volume ISBN-13: 978-0-7172-6245-8
Volume ISBN-10: 0-7172-6245-6

**Library of Congress
Cataloging-in-Publication Data**

Nature's children. Set 1.
    p. cm.
  Includes index.
  ISBN-13: 978-0-7172-8080-3
  ISBN-10: 0-7172-8080-2
  1. Animals--Encyclopedias, Juvenile.
  QL49.N38 2007
  590--dc22

                    2007018358

Printed and bound in China

**PICTURE CREDITS**

**Front Cover**: Nature PL: Ingo Arndt.

**Back Cover**: Nature PL: Ingo Arndt,
Andrew Cooper, Martin H. Smith;
Shutterstock: Dan Briski.

**Alamy**: Alaska Stock 41, Rick and Nora
Bowers 13, Neil Hardwick 34, Juniors
Bildarchiv 30; **FLPA**: Sumio Harada/Minden
Pictures 42; **NHPA**: Stephen Dalton 22;
**Photolibrary.com**: Leonard Rue
Enterprises 45; **Shutterstock**: Shironina
Lidiya Alexandrovna 4, 38, Dan Briski 21,
Peter Clark 17, John Czeke 18, Anita Huszti
2–3, 33, JD 26–27, Gail Johnson 9, Hway
Kiong Lim 10, Bruce MacQueen 37, Rick
Parsons 14, Margaret M. Stewart 6; **Still
Pictures**: Bios/Vernay Pierre 29, Suzanne
Danegger 5, 46.

# Contents

# FACT FILE: Squirrels

| | |
|---|---|
| **Class** | Mammals (Mammalia) |
| **Order** | Rodents (Rodentia) |
| **Family** | Sciuridae (Squirrels) |
| **Genera** | Gray squirrels and many other tree squirrels (*Sciurius*); North American red squirrels and chickaree (*Tamiasciurus*) |
| **Species** | There are several species of gray and red squirrels |
| **World distribution** | Tree squirrels are found in parts of Europe, Asia, North America, and South America |
| **Habitat** | Anywhere with trees, such as woodlands |
| **Distinctive physical characteristics** | Furry with a long, thin body, short legs, and a bushy tail; large eyes; ears often with fur tufts |
| **Habits** | Active during the day; squirrels sleep in tree hollows or nests of twigs |
| **Diet** | Nuts, flowers, berries, buds, birds' eggs, snails, and other small animals |

# Introduction

There are many **species**, or types, of squirrels. They live on many continents throughout the world. Although they may vary in color and size, most squirrels have a large bushy tail, a pointed face with whiskers, and small forelimbs. Some squirrels, including flying squirrels, live in trees. Other squirrels nest on the ground. As well as eating nuts, which they store for the winter months, they like seeds and vegetable matter, and sometimes they will also eat insects.

**Young squirrels practice climbing.**

A chipmunk is
a member of
the squirrel
family.

# A Large Family

Squirrels belong to a very large family. In fact, there are more then 270 species, or types, of squirrels in the world. Squirrels are **rodents**, like rats and mice. Some squirrels, such as woodchucks, marmots, prairie dogs, and chipmunks, make their homes on the ground. These are known as ground squirrels. Other squirrels make their homes in trees. In this book you will find out about tree squirrels.

There are about 50 species of tree squirrels. They are found throughout the world, with the exception of Australia, New Zealand, Antarctica, the Arabian Peninsula, and the far south of South America. Some tree squirrels are called flying squirrels. Flying squirrels have a flap of skin on each side of their body that runs between the front and back legs. These flaps act like wings. The "wings" allow the squirrels to glide between the trees like a paper airplane. A few flying squirrels live in North America. But the most common tree squirrels in North America are gray and red squirrels.

# Neighbors

Whether you live in the middle of a big city or in a quiet country town, you are never far from a squirrel. You have probably seen squirrels in your neighborhood. They are well adapted to climbing trees and grip the branches with their long toes. The tail is used for balancing. They make huge leaps between trees and perform amazingly acrobatic twists and turns through the branches. Squirrels are easy to hear as they crash around the treetops. Sometimes squirrels chase one another just for fun. At other times they chase one another for more serious reasons, such as fighting over mates.

A red squirrel
scurries up a tree
with ease.

9

A young
squirrel pokes
its head out of
a tree nest.

# Becoming Brave

Fully grown squirrels are bold animals. They scamper skillfully through the trees and across the ground, exploring anything and everything. However, young squirrels are more cautious. They spend most of their time peering out of their cozy nest high in the trees.

When they do venture into the open, young squirrels are **timid**. They rarely go far from their nest. The young squirrels run for cover at the slightest hint of any possible danger. Gradually, the squirrels learn what is safe and what is not safe. They become braver by the day. One day soon, the young squirrels will be grown up enough to face the world on their own.

# Reds and Grays

Red and gray squirrels are very different from each other. Grays are common in North America. One type, the eastern gray squirrel, is found in southern Canada, the eastern United States, and also in the midwestern United States. Another type, the western gray squirrel, lives on the western coast, from southern Canada down to California. Grays live in many **habitats**, or types of places, from woodlands to city parks and backyards. Grays are among the easiest wild animals to see in a city. They do not mind living in crowded places. In fact, gray squirrels prefer cities because they have fewer enemies there.

Cities are also good places for squirrels because there is plenty of food around. People like to feed squirrels with bread and nuts. Perhaps you've done that yourself. Squirrels also steal the seeds and nuts that people put out for birds.

Red squirrels do not live in cities. They live only in forests of fir and pine trees. Most red squirrels live in Canada. But they also live in mountainous areas of the United States.

A red squirrel finds
something to eat in
its woodland home.

13

A gray squirrel gnaws
through a nutshell.

# At Home

Every squirrel has an area it calls home.
**Biologists** call this home range a **territory**.
A female gray squirrel can have a territory
anywhere between 5 and 15 acres (2 and 6 ha).
An acre is about the same size as a football field.
Male gray squirrels have a larger territory.
This area can be as big as 50 acres (20 ha).
A male's territory often overlaps with the
territories of several female gray squirrels.

Gray squirrels are not fussy about other
animals coming in and out of their territory.
But red squirrels do not like other animals
intruding into their territory. Red squirrels
chase away all other squirrels and birds—any
animal that might try to eat their food! A red
squirrel has a smaller territory than a gray
squirrel, about 2 acres (0.75 ha).

# Chatterboxes

Squirrels are surprisingly noisy animals. Most small animals like to keep quiet and stay out of sight, but not squirrels. They are lively animals and chatter away in the tree tops.

Next time you are in the woods or sitting in the park, listen for squirrels. If a red squirrel is curious about something, it makes a soft "whuck whuck" sound. When a red squirrel is chasing another squirrel away, it lets out a louder "tcherr tcherr" call. As the squirrel calls, it taps its feet on the branch and waves its bushy tail.

Gray squirrels make calls for the same reasons. They make a "buck buck buck" sound, and if they are frightened or are being chased, they screech. They also hold their tail in certain ways to silently communicate with one another.

A gray squirrel communicates with other grays by holding its tail in certain positions.

Gray squirrels aren't always gray. This one has black fur.

# Coat Colors

American red squirrels are named for their coat of red-brown fur. The hair on their belly is white. They also have a white ring around each eye. In summer a black stripe appears along each side of the body. The stripes separate the red fur on the back from the white hair on the belly. The stripes disappear in winter. A single orange stripe then appears, running down the middle of the squirrel's back.

Despite their name, gray squirrels are not all gray. Most grays have patches of reddish fur. A few are almost completely black. Red squirrels have a close relative called a chickaree, which has black fur. Despite the similar colors, the differences among grays and reds (and chickarees) are clear. A gray squirrel is about 20 inches (50 cm) long from nose to tail. That's about twice the size of a red squirrel.

# Changing Coats

Just as you wear more clothes when it's cold and fewer clothes when it's warm, a squirrel must also adjust to the weather. A squirrel's fur coat changes throughout the year. In winter a squirrel's coat is thicker than it is in summer. The heavy coat keeps the animal warm during the cold weather. In spring the thicker coat falls out. A lightweight coat for summer replaces the winter fur. This process is called molting. In fall the squirrel molts again and the summer coat is replaced by a thicker winter coat.

A squirrel's coat has two layers of hair. The inner layer, or underfur, is made up of short thin hairs. The underfur acts like a blanket, trapping air and keeping the squirrel's body warm. The outer layer is made up of thicker and longer hairs called guard hairs. They stop snow and rain from reaching the underfur. That keeps the squirrel dry and warm.

In winter a red squirrel's fur gets thicker to protect it from the cold.

21

Using its tail
to steer, a red
squirrel leaps from
branch to branch.

# Acrobats

Squirrels are among the best climbers in the animal kingdom. Squirrels use their long claws to cling to the bark of trees. They also have flexible feet. Squirrels can twist and turn their feet to get a grip in almost any position. Squirrels can hang from their hind feet and even climb down a tree trunk head first! In winter, tree branches are often icy. To help stop squirrels from slipping, hairs grow on their feet, so they grip better.

Squirrels can travel a long way without having to come to the ground. When it is time to move from tree to tree, squirrels take a giant leap. As they glide through the air, the squirrels use their tail as a rudder. That way, they are able to steer to a safe landing site. Squirrels can also jump to the ground. They spread their legs widely and use their body as a parachute to slow the fall. Squirrels use this method to drop down as much as 30 feet (9 m) without getting hurt.

# On the Ground

Squirrels have large eyes and excellent eyesight. Good vision helps them figure out where all the branches are and exactly how far to jump. When squirrels are in the treetops, sharp eyesight helps them see food, **predators**, or rivals far below on the ground.

Squirrels often travel down to the ground, especially in areas with few trees. Jumping between widely spaced trees is risky. In areas where the trees are less dense, squirrels climb down and scamper across the ground. Gray squirrels that live in areas without many trees, such as parks and yards, spend a lot of time on the ground. However, they do not stray too far from a tree. If danger threatens, squirrels dash up the trunk to the safety of the branches.

# Keeping a Lookout

There are many hungry predators that hunt for squirrels. Squirrels have to keep an eye out for coyotes, foxes, skunks, raccoons, wolves, bobcats, and large hunting birds, such as hawks and owls. A squirrel's deadliest enemy is the weasel. These agile killers can climb just as well as squirrels. Fortunately for squirrels, weasels are not good jumpers.

Squirrels escape from predators by dashing through the branches or leaping to the safety of another tree. But that might not be enough to dodge a hawk or an owl. To avoid capture by their winged enemies, squirrels have to find a place to hide, such as a hollow or thick tangle of branches. Squirrels know every good hiding place in their territory. That way they always know where to head when under attack.

A squirrel's big eyes on each side of its head enable it to see a wide area.

# Tree Houses

Squirrels build nests high in the treetops. In winter a squirrel builds a snug nest in a dry hole in a tree. The hole might be a hollow formed where a branch has fallen off. Or the hole might be one made by a woodpecker. Squirrels **nurse** their young in the nest. Red squirrels sometimes make a nest on the ground under a pile of rocks.

In summer squirrels prefer to camp out in the open. They build a ball-shaped nest of twigs and leaves in a fork between two branches. This type of nest is called a **drey**. From below, a drey looks like a pile of leaves. But it is actually a carefully woven home that keeps the squirrels protected from the wind and rain.

A drey is lined with pine needles or dry leaves to make it as warm as possible. Each red squirrel builds its own drey. Gray squirrels like to live in groups. As many as six adults cram into one drey.

A squirrel's nest looks much like a messy bird's nest.

A red squirrel licks its tail clean.

# Keeping Clean

It is important for any animal to keep clean.
Squirrels spend a long time **grooming**. As well
as cleaning the fur, the squirrels' rough tongue
combs out any tangles. Licking the fur also cools
the squirrels in hot weather. They do not sweat
to keep cool, but after licking, the saliva left on
the fur dries (evaporates), cooling the animal.
Squirrels also comb dirt and bugs from their
hair using their **paws** and claws. Clean and fluffy
fur is better at keeping a squirrel warm and dry.

Even though squirrels keep themselves clean,
their nests are another story. They do not bother
to leave their nests when they have to relieve
themselves. Their nest soon gets very smelly.
Instead of cleaning out the dirty nest, squirrels
leave and build a new one.

# Happy Days

At sunrise, squirrels leave their nest and get something to eat before beginning the chores of the day. These chores can be anything from gathering material for a new nest to stockpiling food for winter.

By midday, the squirrel is ready for a rest. If the weather is nice, the squirrel stretches out in the sunshine. Otherwise, the squirrel heads back to its nest for a nap. As evening approaches, the squirrel gets busy again. It looks for a final meal before going to sleep for the night. Just like you, a squirrel does not want to go to sleep hungry. If it wakes up hungry, it might pop out in the moonlight to look for a snack.

A red squirrel takes
a nap during the day.

A red squirrel
buries a supply of
nuts for the winter.

34

# Nuts about Nuts

Squirrels are just nuts about nuts! They like nuts because they are easy to store for winter and they are a good source of nutrition. Squirrels bury nuts all over their territory. These supplies provide the squirrels with food throughout winter. Not all of the buried nuts get eaten, though. Nuts are large seeds. Many of the buried nuts sprout into trees. If it was not for squirrels, many forest trees would never have grown!

Other than nuts, squirrels eat mainly plant foods such as fruits and buds. They also eat small amounts of insects and birds' eggs. Red squirrels eat more meat than the grays. Red squirrels also eat snails, young birds, and even mice.

# Sharp Teeth

Squirrels are rodents. Like all rodents, they have four long biting teeth, called **incisors**, at the front of their mouth. These teeth never stop growing. They grow about 6 inches (15 cm) each year. What stops the teeth from sticking out of the squirrel's mouth like tusks? The top and bottom teeth grind against each other when the squirrel gnaws. This grinding wears the teeth away and keeps them from overgrowing. It also keeps them razor sharp. Tree squirrels' sharp teeth and powerful jaws allow these rodents to crack the toughest nutshell.

Squirrels also like to keep their teeth clean. They spend up to an hour each day cleaning them. When a squirrel chews a twig, the wood inside the twig is crushed into tough fibers. These fibers act like dental floss, removing bits of food and nutshells stuck between the teeth.

With their long fingers, a squirrel's paws look a lot like human hands.

A red squirrel searches for food in winter.

# Through the Winter

Many types of ground squirrels, such as woodchucks, **hibernate**. They are inactive or asleep through the whole winter. Instead of feeding, they survive on energy stored in a layer of fat around their body. Tree squirrels, such as grays and reds, do not hibernate. They stay in their nest only during cold weather. The rest of the time, they are out and about, looking for available food. In a snowy woodland, there is not much for a squirrel to eat. However, squirrels plan ahead. Each fall, they store nuts and other foods that will help them though winter.

Squirrels bury nuts with a hard shell one by one. They also store pine cones above ground in small heaps. Some heaps contains hundreds of cones. Squirrels store softer food, such as fruits, in the treetops. The squirrels often put fruits in forked places between branches. There, the fruits are left to dry out. Dried fruits stay edible longer than fresh fruits. The dried fruits offer the squirrels another food source in winter when fresh fruit is not available.

# Finding a Mate

Squirrels **mate** as the worst winter weather comes to an end. Gray squirrels mate in January. Red squirrels live farther north than grays. There, the harsh winter weather lasts longer. Red squirrels, therefore, do not start breeding until the end of February. Mating at these times ensures that the young are born at the start of spring. In spring, there is plenty of food for both the parents and babies. If they mate early enough, some squirrels will mate again in summer. These squirrels will raise a second family before winter arrives.

Sometimes, several males chase one female. The males jostle for position. The stragglers soon start to give up. Eventually, a single male is the clear winner. He then mates with the female squirrel.

A male and female squirrel leave their tree-hole nest at the same time.

A mother squirrel nurses her two-week-old babies.

# Giving Birth

After mating, a male might stay in the female's nest for a little while. By the time the babies arrive, he will have left. The female prepares her nest for the new arrivals by lining it with strips of bark and leaves. That makes the nest warm and dry.

Baby squirrels are born about six weeks after their parents mate. Red squirrels produce a **litter** of about four young. But sometimes there might be as many as eight in the litter. Gray squirrel mothers tend to have smaller litters.

Baby squirrels are born without fur or teeth. Their eyes are tightly closed, and they cannot hear anything. Newborn red squirrels are about 3 inches (7 cm) long. Baby gray squirrels are twice this length.

# Raising the Young

For the first few weeks of a squirrel's life, the only adult the baby knows is its mother. She chases all other squirrels away if they approach the nest. That includes the babies' father. The mother squirrel is also always on the lookout for predators. Her young would make an easy meal for them. If she thinks a predator has spotted the nest, the mother moves her young to a new home. She picks up her babies in her mouth and carries them one by one. She might meet a predator while she evacuates, or leaves, the nest. If so, she puts her baby down carefully and tries to drive away the predator.

One-month-old red squirrels have come out of their nest. They still cannot see at this age.

With practice,
young squirrels
soon become
expert climbers.

# Growing Fast

Squirrels grow up fast. By the age of three weeks, baby squirrels have a little bit of hair on their back. Their bottom teeth are showing through. At four weeks, they can hear. And at five weeks, their eyes open. Newborn squirrels have cloudy blue eyes that are not yet able to see properly. The eyes gradually change to a shiny black. By the time the eyes change color, the young squirrels are able to see clearly.

Like all **mammals**, squirrels live on milk for the first weeks of their lives. That helps them grow quickly. At the age of seven weeks, the squirrels start to eat solid food. By the age of three months, the squirrels give up milk altogether.

# Time to Leave

By the time a squirrel is eating only solid foods, it is old enough to look after itself. The young squirrel leaves its mother's nest and sets up its own home in the trees. In late summer, many young squirrels build nests in trees. These first nests are not very well made. But the squirrels get better with practice.

In fall the young squirrels must prepare food stores for their first winter. They also begin looking for a good place to build a winter nest. Squirrels born late in summer stay in their mother's nest for their first winter.

At the age of about one year, squirrels are ready to mate. Most squirrels live for about five years. Although some lucky ones make it to the ripe old age of 15 years.

# Words to Know

**Biologists**    Scientists who study animals, plants, or other living organisms.

**Drey**    A squirrel's summer tree nest, built of twigs and leaves.

**Grooming**    Cleaning dirt from hairs.

**Hàbitats**    Types of places where animals live. Forests and grasslands are habitats.

**Hibernate**    To go into a deep sleeplike state to survive the cold and hardships of winter. During hibernation, heart rate and breathing slow down.

**Incisors**    Sharp front teeth used for cutting or gnawing.

**Litter**    A group of animals born together.

| | |
|---|---|
| **Mammals** | Animals with hairs on their body. Mammals also nurse their young with milk. |
| **Mate** | To come together to produce young. |
| **Nurse** | To drink the mother's milk. |
| **Paws** | The clawed feet of an animal. |
| **Predators** | Animals that hunt other animals for food. |
| **Rodents** | Animals with front teeth (incisors) that are especially good for gnawing. |
| **Species** | The scientific word for animals of the same type. |
| **Territory** | Area that an animal or group of animals lives in and defends from other animals of the same kind. |

# Find Out More

Books

Murray, P. *Squirrels*. The World of Mammals. Mankato, Minnesota: Child's World, 2005.

Swanson, D. *Squirrels*. Welcome to the World of Animals. Milwaukee, Wisconsin: Gareth Stevens Publishing, 2002.


Web sites

**Squirrel**
*http://animals.nationalgeographic.com/animals/
mammals/squirrel.html*
Information about tree squirrels.

**Squirrels**
*www.enchantedlearning.com/subjects/mammals/rodent/
Squirrelprintout.shtml*
Facts and a drawing of a squirrel to print.

# Index